Aérospatiale/BAC
Concorde

TIMELINES

Matt Falcus

First published 2017

Destinworld Publishing Ltd
www.destinworld.com

British Library Cataloguing in Publication Data.
A catalogue record for this book is available from the British Library.

ISBN 978 0 9930950 9 2

Cover design by John Wright
Front cover image © Damien Thouraine

Contents

ACKNOWLEDGEMENTS...5

INTRODUCTION...7

DEVELOPMENT OF A SUPERSONIC AIRLINER................................9

CONCORDE FLIES...21

ENTRY INTO SERVICE..30

CONCORDE THE CELEBRITY..38

JULY 25, 2000 - THE DAY THAT CHANGED CONCORDE.....................46

THE END OF CONCORDE 50

CONCORDE TODAY 54

THE FUTURE OF CONCORDE..67

PRODUCTION LIST..69

TECHNICAL INFORMATION 71

TIMELINE...72

FURTHER READING...74

ABOUT THE AUTHOR 75

COULD YOU WRITE A *TIMELINES* BOOK?....................................76

Acknowledgements

I would like to thank my friends and family for their encouragement in writing books about the subjects I love and following a passion for aviation. I would also like to thank all of those who have helped source and contribute pictures for this book, including Ron Dupas, Paul Jarvis at British Airways' Speedbird Heritage Centre, Brian Luff at the FAST Museum, and Kate Yates at BAE Systems Heritage Warton.

Introduction

Few, if any, aircraft can claim to have had as much impact on the culture of air travel as Concorde. The name is known the world over and its sleek lines are still instantly recognisable more than a decade after it was retired. Concorde brought glamour and luxury to the jet age and became a symbol of status sought after by travellers keen to experience flying with her.

The aim of Concorde's designers and the two governments behind its development was to change air travel and push boundaries. If their plans were to succeed then the world would be a smaller place, and advancement in passenger airliners would reach new bounds. They undoubtedly were successful in their aim, however the costs of running Concorde turned it into a luxury experience afforded only by the rich and famous and not the masses.

Many factors combined to severely restricted Concorde's success, from worldwide recession and sky high oil prices, to interference from foreign governments and environmental groups terrified of its noise and pollution impact. Concorde turned from a pioneer ushering in a new age of fast travel, which was inspiring lookalike aircraft in its early days, to a one-off supersonic transport with no peers or successors.

Nevertheless, a lack of financial success could not diminish the success of the product, and at the time of its retirement it was still the only supersonic transport aircraft in operation. Concorde would draw crowds wherever it flew; its seats were always sold out, and it created a club of crews and frequent fliers who loved it. What's more, it is still just as popular today as an attraction at museums around the world as it wins over legions of new admirers.

Over the coming pages the story of this incredible feat of engineering and airliner development is told from the days of experimental supersonic flight and aircraft design, to infamous crash which signalled the end of Concorde and its ultimate retirement.

Development of a Supersonic Airliner

Final assembly work underway on the second British prototype Concorde, G-AXDN. This aircraft is now on display at the Imperial War Museum Duxford. (Photo © BAE Systems Heritage Warton)

The quest to reach Mach 1, the name commonly given to the speed of sound, dominated the designs and technical experiments undertaken by early aircraft engineers, spurred in particular by war which was waging at the time. In the 1930s early propeller aircraft had been tested to the point of approaching the speed of sound by being put into a dive at full power, where the effects on the aircraft were noted. These included significant vibration and shaking, to the point where fears about airframes breaking up were very real; nobody knew what would happen when Mach 1 was reached.

Aircraft involved in testing included the Lockheed P-38 Lightning, P-47 Thunderbolt, P-51 Mustang and Supermarine Spitfire which were capable of high speeds, and were able to witness such effects as extreme forces on the aircraft control surfaces to the point that it was difficult to pull out of a dive or control the aircraft. Flutter was also a common experience, and in a number of occasions contributed to aircraft breaking up with the loss of life.

Many claims were made that the sound barrier had been broken, but were usually discounted as inaccurate readings from cockpit instruments. In Germany early jet aircraft such as the Messerschmitt Me 163 and Me 262, which boasted one of the first swept-wing designs, were claimed to have reached speeds of over 700mph in 1944.

Early unmanned rockets such as the V-2 were known to break speeds of up to Mach 4 from their entry into service in the early 1940s. However, the first official manned flight to break the sound barrier occurred on October 14, 1947 when US Air Force test pilot Charles "Chuck" Yeager flew his Bell X-1 aircraft to Mach 1.06 (807.2mph / 1,299km/h). He would become one of the most celebrated aviators in history because of his achievements, and the race was now on to understand and develop the idea of aircraft routinely flying at such speeds, and even faster.

It was accepted early in the pursuit of the sound barrier that aircraft design was important, particularly in the shape of the wings which needed to be swept in order to delay the effects of air compressibility.

The Handley Page HP.115 with its innovative delta-shaped wing. (Photo © BAE Systems Heritage Warton)

Although World War II was now in the past, the ability to fly beyond Mach 1 was an opportunity in the development of new combat aircraft to equip air forces should future wars break out. During the 1950s a number of aircraft types, both for experimental purposes and active service roles, emerged. These included the Handley Page Victor, with a very pronounced swept wing, which officially flew past the sound barrier once, although it was not designed to routinely operate at such speeds. Its stablemate, the Avro Vulcan, would take the wing shape further, introducing what became known as a delta-wing in what was an incredibly iconic design to have a great influence on the Concorde. The design work involved in each successive aircraft brought new understanding into the effects of aircraft shape, engines, and the way pilots flew the aircraft. Thoughts were also turning to whether passengers could be transported at such speeds.

The Avro Vulcan bomber aircraft introduced the delta wing concept when it entered service in the 1950s. The type would also be used to test Concorde's Olympus engines. (Photo © Jacques Trempe Collection, 1000aircraftphotos.com)

Like the Vulcan, which was developed as a bomber, a number of other experimental aircraft emerged with the delta-wing shape. These included the Fairey Delta II, which also featured a new droop-nose concept to allow the pilot a better view of the ground during take-off and landing. In Sweden the Saab Draken included a double-delta wing shape, and in France the new Dassault Mirage IIIa would reach the dizzying speeds of Mach 2.2 in 1958.

The Fairey Delta II, which also featured a new droop-nose concept to allow the pilot a better view of the ground during take-off and landing. (Photo © BAE Systems Heritage Warton)

Many of these early supersonic aircraft were good at flying fast, but could not efficiently and economically fly at both subsonic and supersonic speeds. The Dassault Mirage IV was the first to be developed with this in mind, as its role was of a light bomber which needed such flexibility in carrying out its intended duties.

A Supersonic Transport Aircraft Committee (STAC) was formed in November 1956 which recommended building a supersonic transport aircraft capable of carrying 150 passengers from London to New York at a speed of Mach 1.8 or greater. It also suggested a short-range version capable of Mach 1.2 be developed. Speeds approaching Mach 3, STAC reasoned, would be difficult due to the nature of protecting passengers from the extreme temperatures generated and the expensive metal alloys and titanium which would be required. Duncan Sandys, head of the Ministry of Defence at the time, commissioned a feasibility study into a supersonic transport (SST) in 1959, at the same time announcing the ill-fated TSR2 reconnaissance aircraft which would later be scrapped.

Many designs were put forward, which would settle on the benefits of the delta-wing for its ability to generate enough lift, and would behave acceptably at both subsonic and supersonic speeds. It also removed the need for heavy flaps and slats to be fitted to the wing.

Armed with over a decade of research and experience in developing technologically advanced aircraft capable of impressive speed, and with a firm desire to develop a SST, which it believed to be technically possible, the British government began to seek a partnership with another country. Collaboration with the United States, which was also working on Mach 3

SST designs, was discounted for this very reason – Britain believing it was taking the idea too far into unrealistic and expensive territory. However, near neighbour France already had significant expertise in supersonic aircraft, and had recently developed the Sud Aviation Caravelle jet airliner, which could be beneficial to Britain's own experiences and recent research.

An official agreement was signed between the two countries on November 29, 1962, with a seven article agreement registered in The Hague, which included the responsibilities held by both parties over costs and proceeds from sales. BAC in Britain and Sud Aviation of France would be responsible for building the airframe of the new airliner, with the former constructing the nose, cockpit, forward fuselage, tail section and wheels; the latter would construct the central fuselage and most of the wings and undercarriage. Bristol Siddeley (later Rolls-Royce) and SNECMA would be responsible for developing and constructing the engine powerplants. No collaboration like this had ever been undertaken, and logistically it meant much scrutiny over every minute detail of the project had to be undertaken by both parties, adding to the timescale considerably.

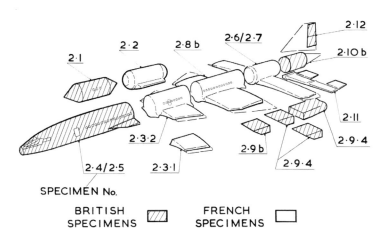

CONCORDE COMPONENT TEST SPECIMENS

Concorde is truly a multi-national project, with parts constructed in both France and the United Kingdom. Each country's manufacturers were responsible for particular component sections, as demonstrated in this diagram. (Picture © Farnborough Air Sciences Trust)

The name of the new aircraft was decided on as Concorde, to reflect the union and friendship between the two companies. Because so much research into wing shape and lift, as well as power plant technology and speed had already been done, there was an ambitious estimate put on the project that would see its Certificate of Airworthiness (CofA) in place by 1969.

Designers had an unenviable task ahead of them which in many cases they conceded would not be fully predictable until the first prototypes were built and tested. Concorde would also present an unusual challenge for the pilots who would fly her, who were used to conventional swept-wing airliners with a smaller wing at the tail. In Concorde's case, the delta-wing removed the need for an additional wing, but meant that it would handle in a much more complex manner. As such, for the first time computer systems were incorporated which would assist the pilot in manoeuvring the aircraft, particularly at speed.

Concorde under construction. The familiar shape of the soon-to-fly airliner is assembled inside the hangar at Filton. A similar scene was taking place in Toulouse simultaneously on the French prototype. (Picture © Farnborough Air Sciences Trust)

The desire for Concorde to fly higher than any other airliner was a useful means by which the indicated airspeed would appear lower than the true airspeed of Mach 2. In fact, indicated airspeed would never exceed 530 knots, which is much closer to the 350 knots flown by conventional jet airliners. This aided pilots in controlling the aircraft. However, the altitude itself would put enormous pressures on the airframe both in terms of heating and cooling and the cabin pressure differential.

Testing the aerodynamic performance of Concorde's nose and cockpit using a special rig. (Picture © Farnborough Air Sciences Trust)

(Picture © Farnborough Air Sciences Trust)

The need to make Concorde a safe aircraft for carrying passengers led to innumerable safety measures and backup systems being employed, with every conceivable eventuality being considered and designed for during the design stage.

Concurrent with the development of Concorde, additional supersonic airliners were in the design phase in the United States, including Boeing's titanium-built SST, capable of carrying 250 passengers, and a Mach-3 capable airliner from Lockheed. These projects would ultimately be abandoned as costs and technical challenges spiralled, however in the Soviet

Union an airliner which very closely resembled the design of Concorde was emerging at the Tupolev Company, known as the Tu-144. It was designed to fly at Mach 2.2, over 6,500km, and was slightly larger than Concorde. Such was its resemblance to Concorde that in in the west it was dubbed *Concordski*.

When it came to Concorde's power plants, the mighty Rolls-Royce/ SNECMA Olympus 593-610 engine was developed. It would offer reheat on take-off and when accelerating to reach cruising speeds of Mach 2, delivering 38,000lb of thrust. In order to feed enough air into the engines, complex movable inlet ducts were developed on the intakes, and to aid deceleration on the ground special buckets were added to the rear of the engines to provide reverse thrust. The Olympus was the most efficient engine in the world at the time.

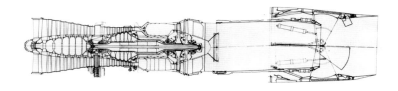

Like with Concorde as a whole, development of the aircraft's engine powerplants was split between Bristol in the UK and SNECMA in France. This diagram demonstrates the responsibility of each partner. (Picture © Farnborough Air Sciences Trust)

The design of Concorde was finalised, having compromised on the extent of its passenger payload, weight, engines and speeds from the original specifications. The use of wind-tunnel testing had been extensive in determining the final shape and expected behaviour of the aircraft under different circumstances. Then, two prototypes were constructed from 1965, one each in Toulouse and Bristol, from parts built in both factories. These aircraft were not intended to be long-range supersonic transports, but testbeds with which the systems and aerodynamic performance could be tested and perfected ahead of full production.

Huge sections of Concorde built in the UK are transported around the Clockhouse roundabout close to Farnborough Airport, bringing traffic to a standstill and drawing crowds on to the street to watch. (Picture © Farnborough Air Sciences Trust)

In December 1967, the first prototype was rolled out of the factory at Toulouse, giving the public a glimpse of the sleek new airliner for the first time.

The British Concorde prototype is almost complete in Filton. (Photo © BAE Systems Heritage Warton)

The moment the world had been waiting for. The first prototype Concorde aircraft is rolled out of the factory at Toulouse on December 12, 1967. (Picture © Farnborough Air Sciences Trust)

Inspecting the tall main landing gear of Concorde following the rollout of the first prototype. (Picture © Farnborough Air Sciences Trust)

Concorde Flies

Concorde 001, the first prototype, takes off on a test flight from Toulouse, France, on December 30, 1969.

The moment at which nearly a decade of development would be put to the test arrived on March 2, 1969 when Concorde 001 would fly for the first time. Crowds gathered at Toulouse Blagnac airport to witness the moment, and television cameras beamed footage around the world to expectant viewers fascinated by the project.

The aircraft, F-WTSS, entered the runway and charged away to the roar of its Olympus engines. At the controls was André Turcat, director of Flight Test Aerospatiale, gently easing her into the skies for a test flight that would last little longer than 30 minutes, where basic controls and instrumentation would be tried for the first time. Landing back at Toulouse, André Turcat announced "The big bird flies!"

On April 6, 1969 it was the turn of the British Concorde prototype 002 to fly. It wore the appropriate registration G-BSST. As at Toulouse the previous month, excited crowds watched the aircraft, piloted by BAC Chief Test Pilot Brian Trubshaw, along with John Cochrane and Brian Watts, depart from Filton airfield near Bristol for its own test flight. On board 12 tonnes of flight test equipment to monitor the aircraft systems. It landed at RAF Fairford a short while later, which has a longer runway and had been chosen as the British base for Concorde test flights.

Pride was high in Europe for the achievements in bringing the futuristic, dart-like Concorde to reality, and passengers were eager for this new era in air transport when distances would pass in a flash. However, Russia's rival Tu-144 aircraft had already flown by the time Concorde first took to the air. The prototype flew on the final day of the previous year, December 31, 1968, as a matter of national pride to reach targets set by the Soviet government. It made its first flight to Mach 1 on June 5, 1969, and Mach 2 on May 26, 1970, becoming the first passenger airliner to do so on both counts.

Concorde's nearest and only rival was the Tupolev Tu-144 which first flew in 1968 and reached Mach 1 for the first time in June 1969. It would suffer a number of setbacks and was ultimately unviable as a transport aircraft.

Whilst the Tu-144 resembled Concorde in many ways, it was a very different aircraft which was capable, on paper, of slightly more but would not fulfil its potential. Rushed to enter service in time for the 60th anniversary of the Communist revolution, the inaugural flight took place from Moscow to Alma-Ata with the cabin interior unfinished and the prototype aircraft having performed less than a thousand hours of testing.

The programme would suffer relentless problems with its design, and at the Paris Air Show in June 1973 the first production aircraft, CCCP-77102 entered an extreme manoeuvre causing it to break up in flight and crash in front of the watching crowds, killing fourteen people in total.

Limited passenger services commence within Russia in 1977. However, following another crash the Tu-144 was relegated to carrying mail and freight across the country before it was finally transferred to airborne testing and research roles in 1983.

Unlike the Tu-144, the test programme of Concorde ran into many thousands of hours for each of the two prototype aircraft. However, on the ground the project was running into criticism from those concerned by a multitude of potential problems that the aircraft was raising. The cost of the project was running to hundreds of millions each for both France and Britain, not helped by inflation during the 1970s. On environmental grounds critics complained at the amount of pollution emitted, including noise pollution and fears over the sonic booms caused when passing the sound barrier, and the increased noise compared to standard jets when Concorde was taking off. Subsequent development of spade devices to counter the noise of the engines on take-off counteracted this claim, as did the revolutionary computer technology which allowed the engines to reduce noisy jet efflux without losing thrust during the take-off stage.

Alongside the prototype flight tests, full-size mock-up fuselages of Concorde were built at Farnborough and Toulouse to undergo testing to simulate an entire life cycle through repeated heating and cooling tests and pressurisation, looking for fatigue issues. Similarly, around 20,000 cycles of the landing gear were performed to prove their strength.

British and French Concorde prototypes sit outside the BAC Flight Test Centre at Fairford, UK during the aircraft's testing phase. (Picture © Farnborough Air Sciences Trust)

Focus shifted to speed. The range and efficiency of the aircraft was tested up to Mach 1 in October 1969, and Mach 2 in November 1970.

Each flight incorporated different power settings and even the effects of losing engines and flying at unusual attitudes.

Two additional, pre-production Concordes were built, one each in Britain and France, and route-proving test flights were undertaken. A French Concorde flew to Dakar in Senegal, and then on to South America. This prototype aircraft did not have the range to fly the journey non-stop, which disappointed some potential customers, but it was promised that production aircraft would have the range.

Focus shifted to showing off Concorde to prospective customers, with examples visiting air shows and airlines around the world. British Airways and Air France had already committed to buy seven of the aircraft each, but if Concorde was to become a commercial success it needed to secure orders from major airlines around the world who were keen to introduce supersonic transport to their fleets. The first major tour was to Australia, followed by the Far East, South and North America. Airlines showed interest, with options for 70 aircraft being held by the manufacturers before a single production example had been built

However, a new battle had arisen in the United States, which had abandoned its own SST plans in 1971, but was now refusing to allow Europe's Concorde permission to fly to its airports over noise concerns. This posed a significant problem for sales in the country, with major airlines already having secured options on Concorde orders.

Seen on September 8, 1972, is British prototype G-BSST performing a fly-past at Warton in Lancashire. (Photo © BAE Systems Heritage Warton)

Nevertheless, testing continued apace, with cold weather trials in Fairbanks, Alaska, during which the Air France Concorde was left for 36 hours on the frozen tarmac and then flown; crews had one minor issue when they couldn't open the door which had become iced shut! Next came warm weather trials in Mexico, and contaminated runway trials back home. The Certificate of Airworthiness was finally granted in 1975, with the first production models now under construction. These featured updates benefitting from the many hours of testing, as well as the full anticipated range and improved Olympus engines.

With the two main manufacturing sites at Bristol and Toulouse both providing parts for the simultaneous production lines, a logistical problem had arisen early in the process where these outsized loads needed to be transported from one site to the other. Initially the fleet of large Shorts Belfast aircraft used by the Royal Air Force were press-ganged into service to carry parts, in addition to sea and road transportation. Later, a fleet of Super Guppy transport aircraft, based on the military variant of the Boeing 377 Stratocruiser fuselage, was developed by Aero Space Lines. It proved ideal in allowing Concorde production to carry on hundreds of miles apart, and would later prove invaluable in the emergence of the new Airbus consortium.

The final assembly line at Toulouse in 1975 showing production Concordes for both Air France and British Airways nearing completion. (Photo © BAE Systems Heritage Warton)

Concorde's narrow cockpit housing the Captain, First Officer and Flight Engineer. The latter was a much more hands on job on Concorde, with jobs including managing the aircraft's centre of gravity through fuel management.

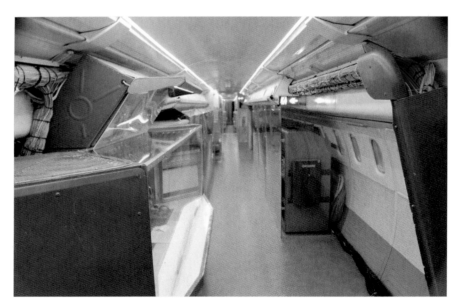

Test equipment onboard the second Concorde to fly, F-WTSB, which is now on display at the Aeroscopia museum in Toulouse.

The second prototype aircraft, 002, at the new £400,000 running base on September 12, 1968. (Photo © BAE Systems Heritage Warton)

Concorde 01 pre-production aircraft after completion of resonance tests at Filton. Seen on April 29, 1971 with tow truck in front of its hangar. (Photo © BAE Systems Heritage Warton)

British Concorde prototype G-BSST approaches Farnborough on September 12, 1974. By now the aircraft was less than a year from achieving its certificate of airworthiness, and had successfully completed test flying which took it to Mach 2. (Picture © Farnborough Air Sciences Trust)

The public is allowed a chance to get up close to British Concorde prototype G-BSST.

Entry Into Service

The British Airways flagship Concorde, G-BOAC, powering away on one of the early commercial flights following the type's entry into service in 1976.

Air France and British Airways had agreed to purchase seven Concorde aircraft each, and worked hard to coordinate the entry into service of the type from their respective hub airports at Paris Charles de Gaulle and London Heathrow respectively. It was January 21, 1976 when the dream became a reality. Air France's F-BVFA (cn 205) departed for Rio de Janeiro via Dakar and British Airways' G-BOAA (cn 206) set off for Bahrain. Each was full of invited guests and dignitaries, and arrival at their respective destinations was followed by banquets and celebrations. The problems with gaining access to New York were forgotten for the time being, as each receiving country gratefully acknowledged the honour of being chosen as the first destinations.

The pressure from the US government and the subsequent 1974 oil crisis had already caused significant customers in Pan American and TWA to cancel their Concorde order options. The cost of running two production lines with only 16 aircraft to build was not sustainable, and yet no more orders were forthcoming and the ongoing ban and media circus surrounding flights to the US was damaging.

Eventually, on February 4, 1976, the US relented and the country's Secretary of Transportation gave permission for both Air France and British Airways to commence scheduled services to its airports on a trial basis to last 16 months. It would allow both airlines to fly once per day to Washington Dulles and twice per day to New York JFK.

The opportunity to show off the aircraft was seized and both airlines planned a joint arrival in Washington on the inaugural service which took place on May 26. The aircraft posed together on the tarmac nose-to-nose under the airport's control tower. It seemed the opposition, which many believed was at least partly based on jealousy, was now in the past and Concorde could begin the role which it had been built for.

New York's John F. Kennedy airport, however, is not as straightforward as Washington Dulles. The impact of noise levels caused by Concorde were carefully considered for the airport's eight possible runway uses (either direction on its four runways), looking at the neighbourhoods and areas of population which would be affected by arrival and departure on each. It was decided that three of the runway uses could never be used by Concorde, and two would be the most desirable. With the latter, a curved departure path led Concorde away from areas of population as soon as it lifted off, directing it out over open water immediately. The runway 31L departure became the most famous of these and was a highly practiced manoeuvre for pilots at Air France and British Airways, both in developing the technique at home, and in simulator practice. It saw Concorde begin its left-hand turn at a hundred feet above the runway and reducing thrust so as to limit the impact of noise on the sensors set up around the airport. Careful monitoring of speed and thrust was continued until away from noise sensitive areas. It was first tried for real with pilots of both airlines on board the first departure from JFK, operated by Air France's F-WTSB on October 20, 1977. Having proved successful, the flagship New York service was commenced by both airlines on November 22.

Although no other airlines had committed to buying Concordes, deals were struck by both Air France and British Airways with other carriers to introduce Concorde services. First, in December 1977, a joint deal between British Airways and Singapore Airlines allowed for the extension of the London to Bahrain service to continue on to Singapore, flying supersonic over the Indian Ocean and avoiding land masses. The Malaysian government briefly banned overflights, which delayed the start of the service until January 1979, but eventually one dedicated aircraft did start the route. G-BOAD (cn 210) was painted in Singapore Airlines livery on the port side, and retained British Airways colours on the starboard side. The cabin crew was made up of staff from both airlines. The route would end after only 23 months when loads began to drop to unsustainable levels due to the worldwide recession. G-BOAD was repainted and the crews would return to operating other Concorde flights, with some being transferred to other aircraft.

January 1979 saw British Airways Concorde G-BOAD painted along the port side in Singapore Airlines livery. The aircraft flew a joint service between the two carriers, linking London with Singapore, via Bahrain. (Photo © Stefan Röhrich)

Another deal was struck between the US low-cost airline Braniff and both Air France and British Airways to bring Concorde services to Dallas, Texas. These would operate as subsonic extensions of the respective Washington routes from Paris and London, making Braniff the only American airline to ever operate Concorde. It had hoped to build on this experiment and go on to buy its own Concorde aircraft to operate on its flagship routes to South America, but yet again the world recession hit hard and load factors were a fraction of that necessary to break even. The operation lasted from January 1979 to June 1980 and had the unusual step of giving the aircraft a new registration which was a hybrid of the British/French and American prefixes. Braniff crews operated these legs.

Once all of the initial run of production Concordes had been delivered, both manufacturers decided to close the production lines as, despite ongoing rumours from airlines that may or may not place orders for aircraft, the reality was understood and no demand was anticipated for additional airframes. At Toulouse the production frames and jigs were completely disposed of in late 1977, whilst in Bristol the British examples were removed and put into long-term storage in case the need ever did arise to use them again. However, on December 31, 1980 the official announcement came that production of Concorde was at an end. The British government had already decided in 1979 to write off the £160m cost of purchasing the first five Concorde for British Airways, paid for by the taxpayers, with 80 per cent of future operating surpluses being paid back by British Airways (which was still owned by the government at the time). Eventually the two remaining production Concordes were delivered to British Airways after hopes of finding buyers were dashed.

Through the early 1980s, particularly in Britain, the financial implications of operating Concorde was continually discussed and monitored by the government and every effort was put in place to reduce the burden by streamlining the operation where possible. It was hoped that the need to repay the government its 80 per cent share could be halted once Concorde had begun to earn more, but the recession at the time had taken its toll. Although occasionally tabled as an option, the idea of grounding Concorde was never seriously considered at this stage.

Air France's network had seen its Concorde aircraft operating an extension of its Washington and New York services to Mexico City from the late 1970s. It had also continued operating to Rio de Janeiro via Dakar, and Caracas via the Azores. However, these services were discontinued in 1982.

Air France started operating an extension of its Washington flights to Mexico City from 21st September 1978. This commemorative cover was produced to promote the event, noting that the entire route from Paris to Mexico City took 6 hours 28 minutes.

British Airways had added Miami as a destination for its Concordes via Washington. It would also introduce a weekly flight to Barbados during the winter months, and Toronto in the summer months during the 1980s and 90s.

However, for both airlines, it was soon realised that their supersonic aircraft had great potential in operating charters for tour groups and special occasions. As a result, Concorde would be seen in all corners of the globe as far afield as Auckland, Buenos Aires, Hong Kong, Los Angeles, Reykjavik,

Lapland, Ushuaia, Johannesburg and many US, UK and French airports, carrying passengers on round-the-world tours, ferrying them to cruise ships, or simply offering sightseeing flights on this most famous of aircraft.

F-BVFB being towed at its home base of Paris Charles de Gaulle Airport. (Photo © Arno Janssen - Jetfotos.de)

Air France and British Airways were the only airlines to take delivery of Concorde aircraft, despite significant interest from carriers around the world during its development stage. Here F-BVFD is seen landing at Paris Charles de Gaulle after a flight from Washington.

In less than glamorous weather an Air France Concorde rests between flights at New York JFK airport.

British Airways supplemented its scheduled Concorde services with regular charters to other parts of the world, as seen here with G-BOAB on turnaround at a desert airport.

Delivered to British Airways on the 13 February 1976. This was the first BA scheme applied to the Concorde and was based on the fleet-wide 'Negus' scheme that was introduced in 1973. This scheme remained essentially unchanged for many years, except the 'British Airways' title became just 'British' in 1980. The final flight of G-BOAC was in October 2003, by which time it had flown over 22,260 hours.

G-BOAA first flew on 5 November 1975 and was delivered to BA on 14 January 1976. By the time of its retirement in 2000, it had flown over 22,768 hours. Aircraft shown in the BA 'Landor' livery that was introduced in 1984 and continued until 1997. The aircraft is now preserved at East Fortune airfield, UK.

G-BOAD was used on a joint Singapore Airlines - British Airways service between Bahrain and Singapore. During this time it carried Singapore Airlines markings on the portside and BA marking on the other side. The service was introduced in late 1977 and operated for 3 months. Services recommenced in January 1979 but were discontinued in November 1980. The aircraft was flown by BA pilots but the cabin crew included personnel from both airlines. The duel Singapore Airlines/BA scheme was applied in late 1977 and remained on the aircraft until 1980.

F-WTSB first flew on 6 December 1973 at Toulouse, France. For the 20th anniversary of the first Concorde flight (2 March 1989), it was painted in a special scheme and rolled-out during the celebrations. Its last flight was on 19 April 1985 from Chateauroux to Toulouse flying a total of 909 hours.

The last scheme worn by the Concorde in British Airways service before they were withdrawn from use. Known as the 'Speedmarque', this scheme was introduced in 1997.

F-BTSD as it appeared during 15-16 August 1995, whilst breaking the eastbound around the world speed record flight. It still holds the record. Previously, in 1992, it had broken the westbound record.

Concorde the Celebrity

Ever the celebrity, wherever Concorde went it drew the crowds, especially at air shows and other events.

There was no doubt about public affection for Concorde from the earliest days, particularly in its home countries of Britain and France. Although it became a means of transport reserved in the most part for the rich and famous, there was no ill feeling about this and people would flock to see the aircraft at air shows or from the rooftop terraces at Heathrow airport.

For those fortunate enough to fly on Concorde it was an unforgettable experience. It was unrivalled in its luxury, comfort and most of all speed. The premium and elite passengers loved the aircraft for all of this, for despite the costs involved in flying Concorde, which could amount to $12,000 for a return ticket from London to New York, it allowed time to be saved and stress to be avoided. This was an important point for businesses who valued the time of their executives. It was often the case that a ticket on Concorde would be purchased to attend a meeting in New York, leaving London or Paris after Breakfast and returning in time for dinner the same day.

Those who flew Concorde became part of the Concorde Club, which was an unofficial badge worn by anyone who had experienced the luxurious airliner. Celebrities and high flying executives were the most common passengers on scheduled transatlantic flights, but on any given flight there were those who had saved up just for the experience – often given away when posing for a photograph next to the digital clock at the front of the cabin which displayed the altitude and speed at which the aircraft was presently travelling.

Anyone who did fly Concorde would be treated to the full on-board experience from the moment they checked in. In each era of the aircraft's operation, from the 1970s to the 2000s, the best in food, drink and comfort was available, starting with the airport lounge which served passengers pre-departure Champagne and canapes.

On any given flight Concorde would carry 21 bottles of Champagne, 17 bottles each of red and white wine, and four bottles of port, which was always popular with passengers on evening flights. Once airborne a drinks service would take place swiftly, but in reality glasses were kept topped up throughout the flight.

Meals were always the best available on any airline, served on fine china with menus rotated every week. At British Airways the menus were planned up to six months in advance, going through a process of elimination which would fuse the most impressive meals with the logistical arrangements of preparing them in the aircraft's cramped kitchen and serving during such a short flight.

The level of service combined with the relative frequency of many of the passengers on Concorde meant that crews were on first name terms with a good number of the fliers on any given flight. Meal preferences and drinks orders were often requested as "the usual" with no hesitation as to what that was. For many regulars, the full meal service was declined in favour of simply ordering a sandwich or snack after an indulgent business lunch in New York.

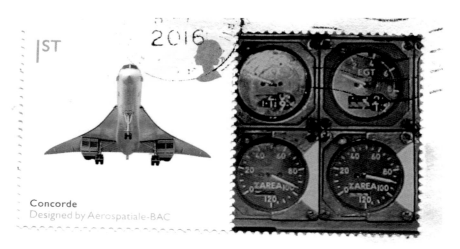

Even as late as 2016, some 13 years after Concorde had been retired, its status was still high enough to warrant it being a feature on a new set of postage stamps issued in Britain.

Crews that flew Concorde were chosen carefully. Whilst it was naturally regarded as the best job in the airline business for both pilots and cabin crew, the vetting process had to be stringent to ensure the level of service, and reliability was not compromised. Therefore, for every vacancy that became available in the Concorde fleets at Air France or British Airways, some 20 to 30 pilots and cabin crew would apply for the position, but seniority usually won over. Any pilot had to be above average and technically very competent, and willing to commit to fly the aeroplane for at least seven years if the airline was willing to pay the significant expense of training them. It is for this reason that there were very few of the younger pilots in either airline selected to switch to the Concorde fleet, and once there pilots tended to remain for the rest of their flying career.

It was an airline within an airline and the interview procedures and selection process were rigorous. Pilots who were successful would undergo up to six months training to fly the aircraft, compared to two months when switching between regular subsonic airliners, such was the demands of flying Concorde to the standard required.

Like many airliners of its time, Concorde required a Flight Engineer, making up the third member of the cockpit crew. This role differed slightly from the same position on other long-haul airliners in that it was much more hands on and saw tasks such as controlling the centre of gravity of the aircraft through fuel management and monitoring the extreme forces experienced by flying at Mach 2.

A typical flight on Concorde, flying between London and New York, would see the crew apply full power and afterburners for takeoff. These boosted the power of the engines by around 25%, but were incredibly fuel thirsty and made Concorde a noisy neighbour, and were therefore switched off after about 90 seconds.

The aircraft would then climb sub-sonically to around 28,000ft. Once clear of land the two outer afterburners would be lit again, followed by the inner pair, creating a smooth transition that passengers could barely feel. Concorde would then accelerate to Mach 2 and climb to between 50,000-60,000ft to cross the Atlantic. The afterburners would be switched off after around 15 minutes to conserve fuel.

The famous droop nose of Concorde was an essential part of allowing the crews to maintain visual contact with the ground on take-off and landing. Because Concorde flew at such a high angle during these slow phases of flight, the nose of the aircraft would obscure any view of the ground and so the pilots would lower the nose to around 5° when taking off, and 12.5° when landing. This kind of versatility was one of the defining attributes of Concorde's design, where every eventuality was taken into consideration and planned in detail.

Concorde's long cabin featured a 2-2 seating configuration throughout. Whilst not as spacious as some of the business and first class seating found on other airliners, the onboard service easily surpassed that found anywhere else in the skies.

Concorde's layout typically included three lavatories for passenger use, however the narrowness of the cabin meant space was restricted somewhat.

Corporate sponsorships of Concorde were common thanks to its overwhelming public appeal. Air France Concorde F-BVFC is seen here with a promotional Motorola Wings sticker underneath the cockpit windows. (Photo © Arno Janssen - Jetfotos.de)

To coincide with a special Concorde 20th anniversary event held at Toulouse in 1989, prototype aircraft F-WTSB was painted in this special "Tricolore" scheme. (Photo © Arno Janssen - Jetfotos.de)

Appearing at air shows around the world, Concorde was flown in formation with the British Red Arrows aerobatic team on a number of occasions. It was a sight certain to draw gasps of awe and promote pride in the country's achievements.

Air France Concorde F-BTSD wore this striking livery in 1996 to promote Pepsi Cola's new can branding. The process was actually done in secret, with the freshly painted aircraft flying from Paris to London during darkness ahead of its unveiling to the world. It then went on to tour Europe and the Middle East, however the aircraft was limited in speed because the blue paint could not dissipate heat in the same way the reflective white paint could.
(Photo © AirTeamImages.com)

Queen Elizabeth II and Prince Philip occasionally used Concorde for royal visits. Here in 1981 they visit Austin, TX.

July 25, 2000 - The Day That Changed Concorde

Captured from an airliner which had just landed at Paris Charles de Gaulle airport on 25 July, 2000, the fate of Air France's Concorde F-BTSC is sealed as it roars into the sky. Flames pour from the wing which was pierced by a piece of metallic debris on the runway. All on board were killed as it crashed shortly afterwards.

By 2000 Concorde had enjoyed 24 years of unblemished service with Air France and British Airways, with no losses or noteworthy accidents to its record, making it arguably the safest commercial transport aircraft in the world. By now it was an established icon of luxury and opulent travel frequented by the rich and famous, but not out of reach of the general public thanks to an increasing use of the aircraft for charter work.

Both airlines took the opportunity of filling the downtime of its fleet by allowing tour organisations to book subsonic flights on Concorde which gave members of the public who wouldn't usually consider the high prices of flying the aircraft on a scheduled flight the opportunity to step on board and experience the thrill of the aircraft and its on-board service.

One such flight was organised on July 25, 2000 by German tour operator Peter Deilmann Cruises to deliver a hundred passengers to join a cruise ship in New York City. The flight would depart on Air France Concorde F-BTSC (cn 203) from Paris Charles de Gaulle Airport at 4.43pm.

The aircraft, which was later discovered to be slightly overweight for the conditions on the day, departed runway 26R a short time after a McDonnell Douglas DC-10 operated by Continental Airlines. A metal strip had fallen from this wide body airliner's engine during its take-off run and was left unnoticed on the runway as no inspection had taken place between the two aircraft departing.

As the Concorde accelerated one of the tyres on the port side of the aircraft ran over the piece of metal at high speed, causing the rubber on the tyre to disintegrate and parts being catapulted upwards into the wing. Whilst the impact itself did not cause a rupture, the resulting shockwave did. Fuel began to leak at the weakest point in the tank, falling and igniting either from the hot engine or an electrical arc in the landing gear.

The air traffic controller first alerted the crew to the flame now jetting from under the aircraft's wing, shortly before the Flight Engineer noticed engines one and two surging before losing power. However, with the aircraft now travelling at over 200 mph the crew did not have enough runway remaining to stop safely and elected to continue the take-off.

This effectively sealed the fate of the aircraft as it was heavy and did not have enough power to climb with number two engine now shut down and number one providing unreliable thrust; it reached a height of around 200ft, passing over the A1 motorway with a trail of flames pouring out behind.

The crew, in their rush to keep the aircraft in the air, transmitted a brief intention to try and land at nearby Le Bourget Airport some two miles away. However, with one wing disintegrating and dragging due to lack of thrust, and another lifting under full thrust, F-BTSC became uncontrollable and rolled almost inverted before nosing into a hotel in the village of Gonesse. In all 113 people were killed, including 109 on board the aircraft and four on the ground.

The crash in Paris sent shockwaves around the world, both for the horrific scenes caught on camera of the aircraft on fire in its final moments, and because of the implications it had on the world's most famous aircraft, which to date had a perfect record for safety.

Following the crash all Concorde aircraft were grounded, both in France and Britain, and wherever they happened to have landed at the time, pending the outcome of the investigation. The cause of the crash was realised fairly early, thanks to the visual evidence from various sources, and in finding the metal strip still on the runway now showing signs of having been run over. How to deal with this obvious weakness in the Concorde's structure would be another matter.

It was a time of reflection for both airlines as to the future of their supersonic flagships. Whilst Air France had been keeping its Concorde aircraft in service as a matter of pride, it conceded that a loss was made on the aircraft every year. British Airways, meanwhile, made millions in profit every year and saw a definite future in its operation.

The circumstances under which the accident occurred were considered unique and highly unlikely to happen again, but it was possible and safety measures had to be taken to reduce any risk. A £17m modification was proposed and implemented which involved adding a Kevlar lining to the fuel tanks of each Concorde, meaning any external rupture of the tank would keep the fuel contained. New tyres were also installed which could withstand high-speed punctures.

A document produced by British Airways announcing the return to service highlighted the safety implementations put in place, reassuring the public that their aircraft was safe to fly and would be even better than before. They boasted a £14m investment in new interiors which included new tilting cradle-action seats which made the take-off and landing more comfortable, new interior fittings which created "a greater sense of space", and new bathrooms.

A test flight was operated by the airline on July 17, 2001 as one-by-one its fleet was modified. On November 7, both Air France and British Airways operated flights to New York, 15 months after the crash in Paris. Both airlines reported fully-booked flights and strong confidence in the aircraft following its modifications.

A grainy picture capturing the Concorde as it struggles for height shortly before crashing.

The End of Concorde

Despite spending millions in order to get Concorde back in the air following the crash of July 2000, inevitably demand would fall in the wake of the terrorist attacks of September 11, 2001. Concorde's days were numbered and the two airlines operating it had a difficult decision to make.

The initial boom in bookings and public interest following the return of Concorde services in 2001 would eventually decline, particularly in the wake of the terrorist attacks in the United States on September 11, 2001, which occurred less than two months before scheduled services resumed.

Although it had been intended that Concorde would fly on for many more years after 2001, especially given the significant investment made in modifications and cabin upgrades to reflect current standards, time was ultimately catching up on the aircraft.

Whilst other classic airliners of the late 1960s such as the Boeing 737 and 747 were still flying, they had undergone several new variations with updated avionics and cockpits, and uprated engines. Concorde on the other hand was still the same airframe using much the same equipment as when it first entered service. Because of the low numbers of aircraft built, there had always been a limited source of spare parts to keep the fleet flying, and no work on new engines had been forthcoming with only fourteen active aircraft. Hence Concorde was incredibly inefficient and expensive by modern standards, and constantly proved a difficult balancing act for its operators who felt it was too significant to ignore, especially given the public interest and prestige of such an iconic aircraft, yet one which was increasingly difficult to maintain and justify its operating costs.

Airbus, the successor of the manufacturing companies Aerospatiale and BAC (through its merger into British Aerospace) was by now responsible for providing parts and maintenance of the aircraft for the two airline operators. It made the announcement in 2003 that it was no longer able to provide spare parts for the ageing aircraft because it was becoming uneconomical to do so. Without such support the aircraft could not realistically continue flying. On April 10, 2003, Air France and British Airways made simultaneous announcements that they would stop flying their Concorde aircraft later in the year. For many it felt too soon, having only returned to the skies 18 months ago.

Ever the publicity hound, Richard Branson of Virgin Atlantic seized the opportunity to trump his rivals at British Airways by offering to buy the Concorde aircraft and continue operating them for many years. His offer of £1 per aircraft (reflecting the price British Airways paid to the British government for the aircraft) was immediately ignored, as was his counter offer of £1 million per aircraft. He would continue to raise his bid to £5 million each, but no deal ever materialised and there was little chance Virgin could have offered much more than subsonic pleasure flights given the lack of spare parts or servicing of the aircraft going forward.

Both Air France and British Airways took the opportunity to arrange flights of their Concorde aircraft as a farewell tour, and played on the significance of the final transatlantic crossings from New York and Washington. The final Air France commercial service was on May 30, 2003. Meanwhile, following a week of its aircraft touring airports in the UK, British Airways' last return New York service was organised for October 24 when G-BOAG departed overhead a crowded shoreline near JFK airport at 7.20am, packed full of celebrities and Concorde frequent flyers.

Two other charter flights had been organised from London Heathrow to coincide with the New York arrival, and all three aircraft converged over the city and landed one after the other for the final time. Again, crowds had gathered to witness the occasion and television cameras from around the globe were relaying this moment in history.

At London Heathrow the final two Concorde arrivals meet nose-to-nose in front of the terminal. Airport workers so used to seeing the supersonic jet pause in their duties to witness the final such time they will see it as part of their daily work.

American and British flags are waved as British Airways Concorde G-BOAG arrives at Boeing Field in Seattle where it will be preserved as part of the Museum of Flight.

Touchdown. This sequence captures the final Concorde to fly as it lands back at its birthplace near Bristol on 26 November, 2003 in front of huge crowds there to witness the event.

Concorde Today

One of the prototype Concorde aircraft is open to explore at the Aeroscopia museum in Toulouse, France.

With the final flights of Concorde completed thoughts turned to the disposal of the airframes. Being such an iconic aircraft there was high demand for them and no chance that they would simply be scrapped. Aside from the example which crashed in 2000, only one other Concorde airframe had been disposed of when F-BVFD (cn 211) was sacrificed for spares in 1992 after it had been restricted in terms of which routes it could operate due to damage from a heavy landing in 1977.

As early as 1989 Air France had signed an agreement with the National Air and Space Museum in Washington DC to donate one of their aircraft to its collection upon retirement. This was honoured on June 12, 2003 when F-BVFA (cn 205) left Paris to take up its new home at the Steven F. Udvar-Hazy Center alongside Washington Dulles airport.

F-BVFB (cn 207) flew to Baden-Baden airport in Germany where it was dismantled and transported by road and barge to the Auto & Technik Museum at Sinsheim. It is now positioned on plinths in a take-off position alongside one of its rival Tupolev Tu-144s, the only place in the world where you can see the two supersonic airliners together.

Raised high in a take-off position, former Air France Concorde F-BVFB is preserved at the Auto & Technik Museum in Sinsheim, Germany.

F-BTSD (cn 213) was retired to the Musée de l'air et de l'espace at Paris Le Bourget airport where it has been kept in a semi-live condition, allowing some of the on-board systems to operate, such as the nose-droop.

Picture © Chris Vondra

The final Air France Concorde flight took place on June 27, 2003 when F-BVFC (cn 209) was flown to Toulouse Blagnac airport for retirement. It was maintained in active condition briefly to assist in any duties relating to the July 2000 crash investigation, but later would be decommissioned fully and is now on display at the Aeroscopia Museum.

One final Air France Concorde, F-BVFF (cn 215) remained at Paris Charles de Gaulle airport where it was preserved on plinths alongside the motorway and active taxiway near Air France's Terminal 2 base for all passing aircraft and motorists to marvel at.

Visible to many from the road leading to Paris Charles de Gaulle's Terminal 2 is former Air France Concorde F-BVFF positioned on plinths as if taking off.

Once the final British Airways flights had taken place their aircraft were quickly dispersed from London Heathrow to new homes around the world. All aircraft would remain the property of British Airways, but would be sent out on indefinite loans to museums which had been successful in bidding for an aircraft, and would be decommissioned to become permanently grounded.

The flagship Concorde (BOAC was the name of British Airways' forerunner, British Overseas Airways Corporation), G-BOAC (cn 204) was flown to Manchester for display at the Runway Visitor Park on 31 October 2003 and is now under cover and open to visitors. G-BOAD (cn 210) made the journey back to New York JFK and was taken by special barge to Manhattan where it now resides at the Intrepid Sea, Air & Space Museum on the Hudson River.

British Airways' flagship Concorde, G-BOAC, is now preserved under cover at the Runway Visitor Park near Manchester Airport. Picture © Darren Wilson

G-BOAD rests on its mooring outside the Intrepid Sea, Air & Space Museum in Manhattan, New York.

G-BOAE (cn 212) also made the journey across the Atlantic to Bridgetown, Barbados – an unusual choice to many, but not unknown as a Concordes destination on scheduled flights. Initially there were concerns over the island's humidity. However, now under cover in an air conditioned building, it forms the Barbados Concorde Experience.

Like Air France, British Airways also sent one of its Concordes to one of the main American aviation museums. In the case of G-BOAG (cn 214) it arrived at Seattle's Boeing Field, where the manufacturer builds many of its airliners, to be put on display alongside such iconic aircraft as the prototype Boeing 727, 737 and 747. The prototype 787 Dreamliner recently joined the collection. G-BOAG was the British Airways Concorde with the lowest flying time, at only 16,239 hours over 5,633 flights, having been grounded for a number of years due to problems with its hydraulics. It was only repaired when demand for charter flights grew significantly and the airline needed extra capacity.

Since moved under cover, G-BOAG has been a star attraction at the Museum of Flight near Seattle since it was retired. It is one of three Concordes on display in the United States.

Meanwhile G-BOAA (cn 206) would undertake the most interesting journey to its new home. It had last flown in August 2000 and was scheduled for maintenance when the Concorde fleets were grounded. Dismantled at Heathrow, it was taken on a trailer to the River Thames and then sailed through central London on a barge, pausing outside Big Ben and the Houses of Parliament, before travelling up the east coast of Britain to the Museum of Flight at East Fortune, near Edinburgh, where it was reassembled and opened to the public. Her final journey was at a leisurely 3mph over farmers fields to reach the museum site.

G-BOAA poses in front of the Houses of Parliament as she makes her way to Scotland via the River Thames. Photographs © Vin Man

Finally G-BOAF (cn 216) would perform the final flight of any Concorde when it departed Heathrow on November 26, 2003. After performing a low pass over another marvel of British engineering, the Clifton Suspension Bridge, the aircraft landed at Bristol Filton airport where it had been constructed in 1978. The airport would later close, however the new Bristol Aerospace Centre has been constructed to house the aircraft and tell the story of aerospace manufacturing at the site.

The last Concorde to fly, G-BOAF, is now inside a new £19m hangar at the former Filton Airport. This forms a part of the new Aerospace Bristol heritage museum. See www.aerospacebristol.org (Picture © Aerospace Bristol)

One aircraft, G-BOAB (cn 208) remains at London Heathrow and has also been deactivated. Attempts to find a permanent home, from Dubai to the ceiling of the airport's Terminal 5 have all fallen through and it remains an echo of the past amongst British Airways' maintenance areas, having been handed over to the Heathrow Airport operator January 2004. Club Concorde, in addition to working on a return to flight (see later) also plans to put G-BOAB on display next to the London Eye in central London as a tourist attraction.

In addition to the operational aircraft, all four prototype Concordes are also preserved at museums in Britain and France. F-WTSS (cn 001), the first Concorde to fly, is on display at the Musée de l'air et de l'espace at Paris Le Bourget alongside F-BTSD, whilst F-WTSA (cn 02) has appeared in a number of different colour schemes on display at Musee Delta alongside Paris Orly airport.

F-WTSB (cn 201) is on display with its test equipment on board in the Aeroscopia Museum at Toulouse, where it was built in 1973.

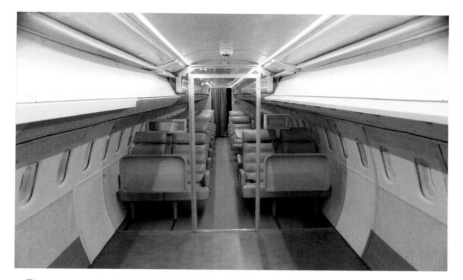

The interior of prototype F-WTSB at Toulouse includes test equipment and original seating.

The first British Concorde to fly, G-BSST (cn 002) is preserved at the Fleet Air Arm Museum in Yeovilton, Somerset, and the second test aircraft, G-AXDN (cn 02) is at the Imperial War Museum at Duxford, Cambridgeshire.

G-BSST on display at the Fleet Air Arm Museum at Yeovilton. Picture: copyright: Trustees of the National Museum of the Royal Navy

The second British prototype, G-AXDN, was retired to the Imperial War Museum at Duxford, Cambridgeshire, in 1975.

A sixth aircraft, G-BBDG (cn 202) was transported to the Brooklands Museum near London by road from Filton in 2004 after being retired from flying in 1981. She had been used in the certification process, and was the first aircraft to carry 100 passengers at Mach 2, wearing the livery of British Airways, but never entered service with the airline. She would later act as a spares source for the active fleet, however parts from the retired G-BOAB have now been used to restore its interior for visitors to the museum to enjoy.

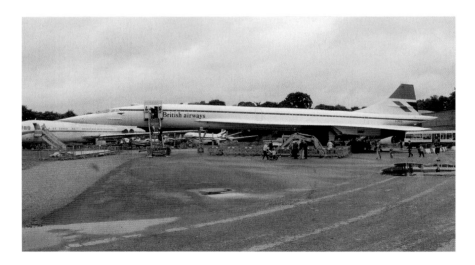

The Future of Concorde

Talk of returning Concorde to flight has existed since the retirement was first announced in 2003, and to many the efforts taken to ensure the airframes remained grounded seemed an unnecessary step to put a hindrance on returning one to the skies. Public appetite in seeing iconic aircraft fly again was never more evident than in the story of the Avro Vulcan which performed for many years following its restoration by the Vulcan to the Sky Trust until its airframe reached the end of its safe use. The chance to see or even fly on a Concorde again would no doubt capture the public imagination and be surrounded by a lot of hype, but it would inevitably come at a high cost.

The former manager of the British Airways Concorde fleet, Jock Lowe, had commented in 2004 that it would take £10-15 million to return a single aircraft to flight. Doing so would be marginally easier if the aircraft was still partially active, with F-BTSD at Paris Le Bourget the obvious example.

In 2015 reports emerged that Club Concorde – a group made up of enthusiasts and former Concorde captains – had secured £120 million in the hope of buying the aircraft at Le Bourget and returning it to flight for use at air shows and on private charters. It hopes to have achieved this by 2019, which will be the 50th anniversary of Concorde's first flight. Much work will be required before then, if the aircraft can be purchased, and regulatory approval gained, yet all with an interest in this fascinating aircraft hope it can be achieved and the roar of its Olympus engines may once more be heard in our skies.

Production List

Construction No	Variant	Registration	Operator	Fate
001	Prototype	F-WTSS	Aerospatiale	Preseved Musée de l'air et de l'espace, Le Bourget, France
02	Prototype	F-WTSA	Aerospatiale	Preserved Musee Delta, Paris Orly, France
002	Prototype	G-BSST	BAC	Preserved Fleet Air Arm Museum in Yeovilton, UK
01	101	G-AXDN	BAC	Preserved Imperial War Museum, Duxford, UK
201	100	F-WTSB	Aerospatiale	Preserved Aeroscopia Museum, Toulouse, France
202	100	G-BBDG	(BAC/British Airways)	Preserved Brooklands Museum, Surrey, UK
203	101	F-BTSC	Air France	Crashed Paris, July 25, 2000
204	102	G-BOAC	British Airways	Preserved Manchester, UK
205	101	F-BVFA	Air France	Preserved Steven F. Udvar-Hazy Center, Washington DC, USA
206	102	G-BOAA	British Airways	Preserved East Fortune, UK

207	101	F-BVFB	Air France	Preserved Auto & Technik Museum, Sinsheim, Germany
208	102	G-BOAB	British Airways	WFU London Heathrow, UK
209	101	F-BVFC	Air France	Preserved Aeroscopia Museum, Toulouse, France
210	102	G-BOAD	British Airways / Singapore Airlines	Preserved Intrepid Sea, Air & Space Museum, New York, NY, USA
211	101	F-BVFD	Air France	Scrapped 1992
212	102	G-BOAE	British Airways	Preserved Barbados Concorde Experience, Barbados
213	101	F-BTSD	Air France	Preseved Musée de l'air et de l'espace, Le Bourget, France
214	102	G-BOAG	British Airways	Preserved Museum of Flight, Seattle, WA, USA
215	101	F-BVFF	Air France	Preserved Paris CDG, France
216	102	G-BOAF	British Airways	Preserved Bristol Aerospace Centre, Filton, UK

Technical Information

Wing Span	83.86 feet / 25.56m
Length	203.74 feet / 62.10m
Height	37.40 feet / 11.40m
Passengers	100
Max Range	3,867mi / 6,223km
Max Takeoff Weight	408,000lb / 185,066kg
Max Speed	Mach 2.04
Cruise Speed	1,353mph / 2,178kmh
Cruise Altitude	51,300ft / 15,636m

The powerful Olympus engines used on Concorde featured buckets at the rear to allow reverse thrust to be deployed upon landing.

Timeline

1941 – First jet engine invented, the Gloster-Whittle (E28/39).

5 November 1956 – Supersonic Transport Aircraft Committee (STAC) formed.

August 1961 – Handley Page HP 115 first flight.

29 November 1962 – Agreement signed between Britain and France at The Hague to develop Concorde.

13 January 1963 – President de Gaulle uses the name 'Concorde' for the first time.

June 1963 – Orders announced by Air France, BOAC and Pan American.

July 1964 – First test run of Rolls-Royce Olympus 593D engine.

April 1966 – Final assembly of Concorde 001 prototype.

August 1966 – Final assembly of Concorde 002 prototype.

31 December 1966 – US decides to progress with Boeing's B2707-200 SST design.

11 December 1967 – Concorde 001 unveiled to the public at Toulouse.

3 December 1968 – First flight of Russian Tupolev Tu-144.

2 March 1969 – First flight of Concorde 001 at Toulouse.

9 April 1969 – First flight of Concorde 002 at Filton.

June 1969 – Tupolev Tu-144 flies past Mach 2 for the first time.

1 October 1969 – Concorde 001 flies past Mach 1 for the first time.

November 1969 – Concorde 001 flies past Mach 2 for the first time.

24 May 1971 – Funding cancelled for Boeing B2707 SST project.

3 June 1973 – Tupolev Tu-144 crashes at Paris Air Show.

26 December 1975 – Tupolev Tu-144 enters commercial service.

21 January 1976 – Concorde enters commercial service simultaneously with Air France and British Airways.

24 May 1976 – Air France and British Airways commence services to Washington DC.

22 November 1977 – Air France and British Airways commence services to New York JFK.

9 December 1977 – British Airways and Singapore Airlines begin joint service to Singapore.

12 January 1979 – Braniff begins operating extension of Air France and British Airways Concorde services from Washington DC to Dallas, TX.

31 December 1980 – Concorde production officially ended.

26 March 1993 – Former hairdresser Barbara Harmer becomes first female Concorde pilot.

7 February 1996 – Concorde's fastest crossing of the Atlantic from London to New York in 2 hours 52 minutes and 59 seconds.

25 July 2000 – Air France Concorde F-BTSC crashes on takeoff from Paris Charles de Gaulle, killing 113 people.

17 July 2001 – First British Airways Concorde test flight following modifications.

7 November 2001 – Concorde returns to service following modifications.

10 April 2003 – Air France and British Airways simultaneously announce they will retire their Concorde aircraft later that year.

30 May 2003 – Final Air France commercial Concorde service, between New York JFK and Paris Charles de Gaulle.

22 October 2003 – Final three British Airways commercial Concorde flights land in succession at London Heathrow.

26 November 2003 – Final ever Concorde flight as G-BOAF is flown to Filton.

Further Reading

Glancey, Jonathan. *Concorde: The Rise and Fall of the Supersonic Airliner*. Atlantic Books, 2016

Gordon, Yefim. *Tupolev Tu-144 – The Soviet Supersonic Airliner*. Schiffer, 2015

Meredith, Adrian. *Concorde: A Photographic Tribute*. History Press, 2013

Orlebar, Christopher. *The Concorde Story*. Osprey, 2011

Ott, James. *Jets. Airliners of the Golden Age*. Airlife, 1993

Trubshaw, Brian. *Concorde: The Inside Story*. Sutton, 2000

About the Author

Matt Falcus has had a lifelong interest in aviation. He is the author of a number of books on aircraft and airports, and has written for magazines such as Airliner World, Airports of the World and Aviation News. He is the editor of AirportSpotting.com

Also by the Author

Handley Page Herald Timelines
ISBN: 978-0-9930950-1-6

The Herald was an innovative British airliner which started life as a piston aircraft and had to be quickly reimagined to utilise turboprop engines in order to keep up with the competition. This book tells the story of the Herald from its inception through to its entry into service, the airlines that operated it, and the remaining examples today.

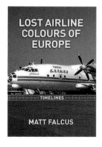

Lost Airline Colours of Europe Timelines
ISBN: 978-0-9930950-4-7

This book traces the colour schemes and liveries of airlines which were familiar across Europe, including national carriers, leisure airlines from the holiday charter boom, and regional airlines feeding our smaller airports. Many airlines in the book have now been lost forever, and others continue in a completely revised scheme.

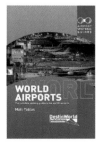

World Airports Spotting Guides
ISBN: 978-0-9930950-3-0

Detailed spotting guides to over 300 worldwide airports. Find out exactly where to watch aircraft, where to take photographs, and what kind of aircraft you'll see there. Includes spotting hotels, museums and other attractions.

Could You Write a Timelines Book?

Authors with specialist subjects are being sought to bring it to life as a *Timelines* book.

Timelines seeks to tell the story of a subject from its earliest days to the present day, or looking at a particular period in time. The series, which relies heavily on photographic and archive images, covers local history, transport, sport and social history. Any subject will be considered.

Get in touch today with your idea by visiting **www.destinworld.com** or sending an email to **info@destinworld.com**